The Magical Listening Tour

You can't get *there*, without going *there*

Paige Francis

*For Steven, David and Scott and **their** endless listening to my exhausting words - thank you*

Table of Contents

Foreword

Nourished Listening
The act of routinely listening to ensure the growth, health and good condition of actions based on shared words. Feeding your ears.

There was a time, in the not-too-distant past, when many technology leaders were viewed as an office version of 'the man behind the curtain' a la *The*

Wizard of Oz and, on the rare occasion their presence was required in a boardroom, the interaction resulted in a bit of confusion, a heaping helping of awkwardness and more than a little post-event dark humor.

Since that time, the evolution of technology elevated its business criticality and, with it, the need for its leader to be strong, collaborative, polished and executive-table-savvy. Today's pandemic doubled-down on the highly visible nature of technology, its role as a facilitator for mission-critical business sustainability and the need for its leadership – chief information officers, vice presidents, chief executive officers – to connect more with increasingly less resources. Efficiency in and effectiveness of technology use comes directly from identifying and reprioritizing need, in real time. To continuously shift technology focus requires knowing and deeply understanding the whole business, as one, amid internal and external chaos.

I have found the highest reward comes from

tackling head-on the assumed risk that often keeps leadership from embracing unscripted events. I call these unscripted events listening tours.

Make no mistake, while this quick read comes from the viewpoint of a modern technology leader and is aimed at career-focused individuals needing to more successfully dial-in to their people network, ***nourished listening*** - or simply listening to understand - is equally useful in parenting, maintaining friendships and life in general.

An investment of time in authentic listening on every front-end can save endless hours of frustration - and time, and dollars, and energy - on the back-end. And, for those that have built trust only to have it lost due to a missed expectation or a single wonky communication, we know rebuilding confidence after a disappointing experience can be difficult-to-insurmountable. Therefore, continuing the listening tour over time ensures actions and decisions remain responsive to and mindful of changing environments.

While the concepts in this book are simple ones, it's important to embrace that simple is subjective. Planning to listen and then actually listening to learn does not come easy to everyone. If the skill isn't innate, it must be practiced, sometimes awkwardly. In those moments, show some grace to those showing up for you and trying something new to be a better partner. In addition, if the struggle is real for you, show some grace for yourself as you learn. Most important things rarely come easy, despite seeming super-simple.

Learning an entire business ecosystem - whether before, within or after a pandemic – requires relationship-building. Authentic, respectful, reciprocal relationships empower a foundation of understanding that leads to an awareness of how the business will likely respond to shifts and moves over time. It also enables a visualization of the interconnectedness – a puzzle, really – of the whole landscape.

We study, we strategize, we whiteboard; yet sometimes we forget a business's most valuable and insightful resource – its people. And getting to know the people develops a more comprehensive understanding. If there are gaps, the people have experienced them first-hand, or heard about them, or even created them!

As a technology leader in higher education, a decade ago my focus on communication, empathy and humble leadership was often viewed as a weakness. Today, here we are. While the art of listening to the community comes as second nature to me, I understand it is perplexing to many. The question on 'how' has been raised hundreds of times over the past year. I'm happy to share my how. Yes, it seems obvious and simple to me. However, that is not the case for all.

Just recently I had a conversation with a higher education executive that was on the cusp of outsourcing an entire technology team. After two open, transparent conversations with internal constituents and a single vendor, he had hope. And he recognized he had just about thrown the baby out with the bathwater. He couldn't get *there*, without going *there.*

We don't know what we don't know. And we won't know if we don't have the conversations.

Much of the thoughts and counsel on the following pages are shared through a lens of normalcy. How I would normally attack a listening tour. It's important to recognize that in the midst of today's remote reality thanks to Covid-19, the ability to gather is much easier to finesse. Virtual engagements are equally effective in starting to build the relationships that bolster instinct and assumptions with clear and current firsthand knowledge.

Once you build trust and start to be known at the leader that encourages feedback and embodies approachability, you will notice the landmines before you step on them and pictures of next steps continuously refocus with increased clarity.

Now how to begin?

Clear Your Mind

First Things First

In order to fully embrace listening tours and all associated concepts, clearing your mind is important. This moment - the right now - is truly a time to forget everything you've learned or assumed about how effectiveness, leadership and success happen.

Of course, you must start projects and finish efforts. You must establish measurable outcomes and keep track of them over time. You must develop policy and procedure, train users and socialize a continuous improvement mindset. You must drive an innovative, resilient culture and instill enthusiasm and appetite for change in others. Everything you do and pursue needs to bolster and further the bottom line and support the overarching strategic plan and goals for the business. Blah, blah, blah. But before all of that...first things first.

The critical component begins well before all of the obvious business *strategery*. It begins at the beginning. It begins with identifying and truly understanding needs and wants. And you can't get *there,* without going *there.*

Repeat after me:
  √ Communication is important
  √ Building authentic relationships is important
  √ Listening is important

To be clear, communication, building relationships and the very concept of listening tours - to empower nourished listening - are not comfortable actions for many; however, all humans are capable of learning how to pull off these collaborative events and benefit almost instantly from the art of a listening tour.

Spoiler: You are clearing your mind because there are individuals - some seemingly successful - that loudly criticize or passive-aggressively mock the value of relationships and listening in overall effectiveness. Clear your mind of that nonsense.

The Buzz Phrase of You

As a prerequisite, think about who you are right now. Self-awareness is important. Recognizing these are extremes while being honest with yourself, which buzz phrase do you most easily identify with:

- *Don't mistake confidence for competence.* Do you instinctively think 'frivolous' or 'fluff' at the mention of listening tour, communication, relationship-building? Is your ego or self-worth tied directly to (finger quotes) more important (end finger quotes) skills that also happen to be your own personal strengths?

- *Don't mistake grace and kindness for weakness.* On the flip-side of the confidence and competence stance, there is certainly nothing weak about the *catch more flies with honey* proverb. A working concept is less about useless flattery and more about building trust by being kind and empathetic. Between building trust and the archaic barking boss, the latter is the weak link in effectiveness, both professionally and culturally.

- *Stay teachable.* Do you fear publicly owning personal weaknesses, yet are open to learning new things to strengthen areas of unknown?

- *I am here for it.* Have you participated as audience for a listening tour, imagine the impact it might have on buy-in from your business perspective and want to learn more?

Whether one of the above buzz phrases instantly makes you feel attacked (ding!ding!ding!) or you feel like a healthy mix of all four and then some, there is no wrong answer. But it's important to recognize where you are and who you are - your inside voice - to move forward, to recognize what baggage you might need to unload and, most importantly, how deeply you can commit to learning something new.

The good news? Anyone can learn how to pull off a successful listening tour. There's no magic to it. Anyone can easily fold the art of the listening tour into their bag of professional tricks. It might start slow, feel feigned, exude an initially awkward feel, but that's ok. Start where you are. Comfort levels and execution will improve over time.

In addition, learning how to listen to the masses is a solid investment. It's endlessly bullish. Listening tours will never go out of style or lose effectiveness. Why? Well first off, because people want to be heard. Listening tours keep the user at the core of the why, ensure what is developed most closely hits the real need and they open lines of communication and feedback that deepen connectedness even when you are 'off the road'.

Those moments between tours? If you are sincere in delivery, the audience will remember who to contact and how because they have confidence it will result in improvement.

Know Your Audience

Skills like relationship building, empathy and productive self-awareness often go hand in hand. For those that struggle with the more people-centric skills, understanding the importance of and respect for how differently individuals receive others is critical. At all times it is important to respect the differences and preferences of others.

Think about how you like to be approached. How do you develop relationships?

- If you are a technology-leaning leader, do you measure respect by the depth of technical knowledge?

- If you are a financial-leaning leader, do you bond more with colleagues over long P&L conversations?

- If you are a sales-leaning leader, are you always trying to get that customer in that car today?

Listening tours - while they certainly drive success for you - ***are not about you.***

Listening tours are not about you.

Shelve what only works for you. Chances are, you're not always - or even most often - going to be speaking with 'your people'. On a listening tour, you'll be speaking almost exclusively to colleagues outside of your department. Read: Your most-valuable audience is the audience staunchly outside both your comfort zone *and* your area of expertise.

You will need to rise above what you know and

elevate yourself to the state of **we**; where discussions are bigger than you.

Industry jargon and deeply specific conversations are not leadership, they are management. Listening tours are for leaders.

Always know your audience. Know who is in the room. Remember at the highest level, you are there to listen to them. Everything they share has value. Maybe not today or tomorrow, but keeping a mental note of all the words is important while also dissecting out the pieces that apply today. It will come out differently than you might share yourself, by design.

Again, you are listening to and for others.

A New Way of Life

Despite the simplicity, listening tours are not natural for many. The good news is they are learnable and doable. Who this book won't work for? Only those that refuse to grasp the value of including diverse opinions and outlooks in decision-making and planning. Authenticity can't be faked long-term with listening tours.

This is a lifestyle, not a task. These are relationships, not superficial interactions.

Everything you've learned prior to today will be re-infused into your how. The difference is that, for now, we will focus on elevating approachability, empathy and genuine communication aimed to make and maintain a positive impact.

We are embarking on more than a soft skills adventure. Enjoy the ride.

Listening Tour Logistics

What is a Listening Tour?

Well, it's the most basic thing in the world. It's taking time to listen to others. Routinely. It's understanding that nourished listening takes careful planning, much forethought and absolute intentionality. The coordination of the whole picture makes me think of the gentleman in Jurassic Park (minus the disastrous results, of course) and his 'spared no expense' line. Except, in this case, that expense is not financial; it's investment in professional grace, engagement, time.

A listening tour is simply where you listen, routinely, for the purpose of learning. In most instances, you are learning how to do your job better, how to work more efficiently and, ultimately, eliminate wasted resources by delivering what is needed, the first time.

When to Start

Is there a best time to start a listening tour? In most instances, the answer is yes. And that time is now.

Every second a listening tour is moved to a back-burner, that is a second lost and not spent building relationships designed to discover the importance epicenter. Listening tours benefit all ladder rungs.

Examples:

- If you are a leader, it best serves your staff to model inclusive, authentic, visible efforts designed to unify and continuously improve service.

- If you are not a leader today but on a path to leadership, building relationship-building into your skillset is a worthwhile investment. In addition, refining how you communicate with peers, colleagues and management instills self-confidence and builds confidence in you by others. Communication and buy-in is always a critical skill.

- If you are not a leader and have no interest in being a leader, that's fine. But you are doing a job and you have tasks to complete. There is little more frustrating than completing a task only to find out it missed the mark, either slightly or entirely. Those misses are often identifiable long before the development starts. A task-focused listening tour up front leads to fewer gaps and less time spent fixing what didn't need to ever be broken.

Let's face it, many have extensive knowledge and industry expertise. But if you don't know who you are serving and haven't included *the whole* in your roadmap development - instead you've blindly devised a plan for the parts based on historical experience or current assumptions - you are baking in future gaps that will need to be addressed down the road. (In technology, that often leads to what we call *technical debt*.) While that is neither efficient nor valued, it's also professionally damaging. "Why didn't you ask me to begin with? Yet another example of how silo'd we are."

So, we're starting now. But-but-but...! Calm down. Keep in mind, the launch process also includes the period of time where you are fleshing out the who, what, where and how. Listening tours do take planning, but, as Mark Twain famously said, "The secret to getting ahead is getting started." So, let's get started. Now!

But, where do I start?

Where to Start

Right here. You start wherever you are. Certainly, it's easier to introduce the concept of a listening tour when you enter a new company or a new position. This is especially true if you've painted yourself into a silo and never exhibited collaborative behaviors.

For example, I worked with a colleague who had been working at my new-to-me institution for almost two decades. When I joined, I started on a listening tour. After a few months, relationships and trust were built.

One thing I've started doing in the listening tour process is recognizing that I can't be the only person developing relationships. And knowing that this listening tour process isn't comfortable for everyone, I tend to bring my peers along, guide them in, as the opportunity presents itself.

In this instance, I folded a colleague into a conversation with one of the university deans. When he introduced himself, she asked, "So, how long have you been at the university?" When he responded with 20 years, learning he was a member of the leadership team, she pointedly asked, "Well why haven't I ever heard of you?" And it was asked with a bit of snark.

Of course, he could turn around and ask the same, but if you are in a position of service or support, people should know who you are.

We are all at different places - theoretically and physically - in our lives and careers. Whether it's an introduction or a reintroduction, now is the time to start. If you get the question, "Why now?" Or even the saucier, "Why are you suddenly interested in us now?" - honesty remains the best policy.

There's no shame in owning that you've recognized how important dialogue matters and that you are hoping to deepen campus - or business, or life, or personal - relationships. You can't best support without knowing who you're supporting. Ideal answer? "I'm disappointed in myself to have not taken this step sooner. How can I be effective if we don't work together in defining what effectiveness truly means?"

It's not only okay to own past slights - whether intentional or unintentional - it's reality and it's wholly guileless. And when you show honesty and hold yourself accountable for historical 'misses', it exhibits humility and caring for others.

How to Start

Review your calendar. Is it two weeks before a holiday break? Is it the business time of the year for many? Start at a time that you recognize is mostly unfettered by business requirements. In accounting, this will *not* be tax season. At Fed-Ex, this will *not* be between Thanksgiving and Christmas. In higher education, this *will be* in the middle of a semester at a point furthest away from the first day of classes and final exams. In higher education this will also be in the summer for staff, but *not* faculty. It takes thought. And flexibility.

Learning this critical business point is important. If you hold a listening session two days before a holiday break, focus will be elsewhere and the content forgotten after an extended break.

And how will you sell this? Think of your project list. Think of your end goal. Think of your department's positioning within the business.

From a big-picture perspective, input that represents the sentiment of the entire organization, from various perspectives, adds value. In addition to being valuable, including others bolsters buy-in, furthers professional stature and drives a team-oriented culture.

And the invitation list? Who should be included in your listening tour, you ask? To a degree, everyone should be invited. Learn the business.

Who is impacted by your work? As someone leading technology, that answer is truly everyone.

Stymied from your unique vantage point in the organization? Start with an organizational chart. Learn the departments, department functions, the dependencies, their role(s), the impact on people-time-effectiveness, find the intersections, prioritize the business impact.

As a higher education leader, I've recognized several important starting point sources. These might translate directly to your line of business or they might not. In the 'might not' category, think about the roles I'm describing and apply that to the underlying influence that happens across your office(s).

- Department admins
- Faculty
- Students
- Staff
- Academic Leadership
- Administrative Leadership
- Alumni

- Parents
- Donors
- Community

If you've been in a 'business' for ages, you were likely hired for your expertise in that line of business. This is a great opportunity to revisit and relearn. Fresh eyes can eat decades of industry experience for breakfast. Learn to learn fresh. "We've always done business this way" appears to be a dying last gasp. Lead with that if you feel unsure of why you're embarking on this journey.

Frozen with nerves about starting on this? Try with your own team first. A concentric circle approach is an easy starting point. Start from you and work out - your team, your peers, peer teams, all leadership, and so on. In some businesses, the reverse might be true. Start from the outside and work inward. Feeling brave? Start from the outside and inside and work toward the middle.

What's the Message?

And now the message. What is your message? Define your message. If you are just getting started, the message can be as simple as, "I'd like to learn more about what you do to make sure that we are prioritizing our work around your needs."

As an IT leader this is often, "As I start to map out our priorities, I'd like to spend some time learning about what your team does to make sure that our work aligns with your roadmap. It's difficult for me to prioritize in a vacuum; I'd like to learn to make sure we get it right the first time."

Note, this message works whether you've been at a university (or company) for 10 minutes or 10 years.

It's OK to start wherever you are.

Watch the Schedule

Given you've already refined your message (which can be forever fluid) and identified and prioritized the groups/teams to meet with, it is time to coordinate those interactions.

What is your timeline? This is all based on urgency, current state, expectations, even generally accepted work culture.

If you literally have no clue where to start, start anywhere.

It starts with an email:

Hi Jan,

I would love to set up a time to meet with your whole team. No preparation needed, open forum. I'd like to get some insight into your area's current initiatives and how technology might help in any way. Is there an upcoming all-team meeting I could insert myself into or is it easier to just schedule separately? Easy either way.

Thanks much,

Your Name

Department/business unit meetings are obviously the easiest.

However, if you've met someone that has inferred issues or concerns held by an unknown swath of colleagues, you can start with that person. This is an actual email I sent to one such person upon arrival at a new institution.

Hi (Name),

*OK who are my **Queen** Bees to*
target for a bi-monthly gathering?
I met (another name) yesterday
and she self-identified as a QB.
Thanks!

To clarify, the Queen Bee tag was one that was introduced to me. Those with influence and a working knowledge of the underbelly of the university referred to themselves, behind the scenes, as Queen Bees. Her response:

Thank you for reaching out! I
have done some thinking on this
and the "best" admins to give you
the honest feedback you are
requesting. The list below are
department assistants or admins
that are in the trenches with all
things! Financial, Colleague,
scheduling, courses, transcripts,

and hiring forms. Hopefully you
will get some good feedback.

Scheduling should be manageable, meetable and not too aggressive. Regardless of urgency, a listening tour cannot be a sprint. Especially for beginners. The planning is critical for success. The meetings themselves need a comfortable-for-all cadence.

On the backend, you have to bake in time to fully ingest what you heard. Re-read the notes you took or watch the recording again.

In the beginning, I tend to map out the initial listening tour schedule then bounce it up against colleagues - Is this a culturally acceptable pace? Is this too much pressure? I've rearranged the meeting order - does it still translate?

It's interesting to note how much you will learn about the organization, its culture and its teams throughout the whole listening tour journey. It may be surprising to find that at times you may learn more in the planning phase itself. A key thread throughout the listening tour process fabric: the learning opportunities never stop. You will be surprised as those moments rear their heads. You will then begin to look forward to them.

It's Showtime!

Setting the Stage

While this exercise is all about listening, you don't just show up and everyone starts spilling their guts. Well, some do and always will. Those folks may have some insight, but the more valuable feedback typically requires a bit of drawing out. You need to get the people there and, oftentimes, drilling into the legit trouble spots is the most difficult part for folks not adept at pulling information out of people.

Some questions and prompts may need pre-legwork and clearance.

What is the word on the streets? Are there very clear gaps and issues or do small stories keep filtering up discreetly that are painting a picture for you?

Example, communication and transparency are almost always issues in any business. Particularly for information technology units. If you've heard of issues, make sure you share them with the technology team first. 'I've been hearing these things. In order for us to improve, we need to be accountable for possible issues. I will be asking these questions of your colleagues outside of IT. Know I'm doing this to get at the root issues here, not build a case against our people, past work or legacy performance.'

It is important for the department you are representing to understand and believe that improvement requires hearing the criticisms alongside the praise. And, while we want to continue hearing the praise, we really need to tackle the hard things in order to bridge the gaps.

In fact, and I'm skipping ahead a bit, you will likely find on your tour that there may be issues that are legacy assumptions that have oftentimes already been remedied. Reminder: Don't use your listening tour to share updates. Instead, document those legacy issues and use them for quick wins. Use your listening tours to listen.

Laying the Foundation

There should always be an initial communication that precedes the calendar invite. Introducing *the why* and giving a jargon-free warning that a formal meeting invitation is coming always smooths the process.

Let's be real. For those of us working in information technology, supporting a whole business, most of our users and departments don't hear from IT leadership unless something has gone wrong or we are on the verge of implementing a change. A change that, regardless of improvement level, will require time, energy and something new everyone must now learn. (Insert audible sigh, eye-roll, hands in air.)

In addition, these days, trigger declining vague or unanticipated calendar invitations is a real thing. Is this a sales pitch? Is this going to waste my time? Everyone is exhausted.

From the first listening engagement through every following iteration thereof, take the time to lay the foundation via easy introduction. That first one can easily be jarring and perplexing, "Why is a vice president emailing me?"

Make it smooth. Something like:

> *Good afternoon all. If we haven't*
> *yet met, I'm hoping we can fix that*
> *soon! I'm the University's chief*
> *information officer and am*
> *accountable for technology use,*
> *service and support across our*

campus. Shortly I will be sending out a calendar invite for an open session dedicated to {insert department name, school/college name, business unit, student committee, etc.} and I hope you can attend.

I am hearing that there are times where IT isn't 100% meeting expectation and, given our primary role is to facilitate teaching and learning, I'd like to make sure your experience is a driving force in the plan of action we're crafting. Please bring your ideas - the bolder and louder the better - as I plan to listen. Your success is our success and we'd like to make sure we're doing our part.

I'm scheduling this session at a time recommended that most

should be able to attend by your
Dean/VP/Committee Chair. For
those that can't attend, we'll
record the session and post quickly
for your review.

My door is always open. I am
always hopeful for feedback! See
you soon.

Of course, that introduction should feel natural for you. However, delivering it is critically important for participation and to set the overall tone moving forward. Open. Collegial. Hopeful. Capable to embrace and genuinely welcoming of criticism.

Sample Questions

And just like that, it's showtime.

Your event is looming and it's feasible for the first

few sessions - and possibly every single one - there is a sense of dread and, dare I say, fear leading up to go-time.

Note, very few people won't experience an odd sense of discomfort prior to session start. In fact, if there is no moment of nerves, you might need to remind yourself that this is not a *you* show. This is a *them* show. If you're overly confident, be careful. I have experienced over-confident folks who, as feedback hosts, flip to totally dominate the conversation.

Whether this session is virtual or in person, it starts with a brief, genuine introduction. The introduction should be more about feelings of wanting to be a better service provider and less about personal accomplishment. Some quick sample questions to get dialogue going:

- What is working for you from IT?
- What could we do better?
- Have you noticed gaps?
- Have you heard any ideas or creative

solutions from friends outside of our institution?

- This pandemic required a rapid shift to virtual work. What is still missing? What's was or is the biggest pain-point at this time?

It is not uncommon for colleagues to not want to share negative feedback. It can help if you ask questions that allow them to cloak their responses in others' experiences.

One example, "Without naming any names, have you heard of gaps that are impacting others being able to do their work? No example too small. We don't know what we don't know."

These are the softballs. Keep in mind, if these generic questions prompt generic - or no - response, there's more there. Start to dig:

- I've heard that sometimes help tickets get lost in the shuffle. Have you heard of that happening?

- Being new to this environment, I'm used to a bit more collaboration on research needs between faculty and IT. How does this work here?
- As colleagues doing mission-critical work, what is missing from a technology standpoint? What would make doing your work easier?

Again, the first tour can be quite painful for all involved. Especially in environments where listening doesn't noticeably happen. Or, worse, in environments where staff have shared their needs and concerns, yet nothing has been done to address them. Keep pushing.

The Cadence

Throughout the course of the session, keep things moving. Think in advance on how you might keep the dialogue flowing. Know this - if this is foreign territory to the institution, if the business has a history of struggling with transparency and communication - the first session might be awkward and uncomfortable. Continue to remind yourself that this is the beginning of a powerful journey and it's okay for the first session to end early, produce little feedback and feel less than fruitful.

You have one job: *Establish the introduction to a new relationship.*

Pretty much the end. Stay positive, stay energetic, show no disappointment or awkwardness, just plow forward and end with a heaping helping of gratitude and a side of 'this will happen again'.

And always remember, it is perfectly okay to end a session at its natural end point. An early end is ok. "I hope this doesn't upset anyone but I'm thinking I just might be able to give you twenty minutes back." (smile)

The After-Party

Send a thank you. Share the information you captured in the session and seek feedback on its accuracy. Did you get to the crux of the message? It can be easy to miss underlying themes when you are new to listening to understand and/or your audience does not feel that reciprocal trust quite yet.

Regardless, even if you keep it topical for a few sessions, it's important that you share what you heard, seek confirmation that you heard correctly, identify one-to-many improvement areas and deliberately and measurably deliver improvement in those identified areas.

Those already-fixed issues based on years of assumptions and poor communications? Use them as examples of action. "I listened. We fixed based on your feedback. Let us know your thoughts. Thank you!"

Next steps? Communication ultimately connects the dots over time. Imagine these communication points:

- √ I listened
- √ I heard you
- √ I confirmed what I heard was accurate
- √ We developed a plan to improve something that matters to you
- √ We delivered actions for improvement
- √ Look, listening and communicating works!
- √ See you soon!

Of course, this process seems elementary because it is. In our increasingly complex world, it seems so easy to deprioritize the simplest things.

The Comeback Tour

The title of this book is not The Magical Listening *Event*. The concept is not about a one-and-done effort to define the future of needs. You are reading *The Magical Listening Tour* and tour is defined as "a long journey including the visiting of a number of places in sequence, especially with an organized group led by a guide."

While you don't need to officially schedule your listening tour out for numerous years, you do need to map out the tour map internally.

For example, annual engagements as a concept to check back in with the departments, teams or units allow you the privilege to:

- **Share how *their* previous insights directly impacted tangible changes and ask 'Did we get it right?':** This builds confidence, buy-in and ownership. Participants become a part of the roadmap rather than simply as a top-down recipient of announcements.

- **Gather new information in light of today's status:** Capture what has changed, what might work better now that we know what we know.

- **Own mistakes, failures, missteps, blind spots, tone-deaf responses or miscommunications:** This is what authenticity and accountability looks like. *To err is human*, and there is no faster way to drive a culture of improvement than by showing how learning from missteps and obstacles leads to innovation and greatness. Normalize failures as the wonderful growing opportunities they are.

- **Keep the connection with the whole business:** Relationships are built on trust, confidence comes from repeated achievement, connectedness comes from, well, connecting consistently.

- **Experience lightbulb moments:** The more you get outside of your own thoughts, ideas and mind space, the more creative you become.

Whether you use a physical or virtual planner, map out your tour to ensure you stay on top of annual scheduling.

Keep It Fresh

No one has time to listen to a canned speech over and over. Keeping your listening tour fresh is a lot like keeping any relationship fresh. Find new things to share.

Examples include:
- When a business updates its strategic plan
- When a security breach hits national news
- At the beginning or end of something routine (example, a new semester in

higher education)

- Internal or external survey results are compiled
- The company survived an event (examples, minor implementation or a pandemic and anything in between)

You get the gist. It's not complicated. Identify a trigger to justify a touch base. Keep it simple. Keep the dialogue fresh. Folks get exhausted by unnecessary, persistent communications.

If this comes naturally to you, find a small group of diverse individuals and bounce ideas off of them. Would you want to hear this? Run through communication drafts with them. Does this sound authentic? If you have professional spirit animals that you can rely on for brutal honesty, ask them the hardest questions. Is this tone deaf? Do I sound like a self-promoting lackey?

If you genuinely want buy-in, the relationships you are seeking must be reciprocal. Again, you don't need to be an extrovert or a people-person or even engaging. All personalities are effective-capable as long as the messages delivered are honest and the ensuing feedback is genuinely wanted and openly received.

In Closing

The listening tour act itself may seem like exactly that - an act - for some, for an indeterminate span of time. However, unless there is a substantial lack of drive to learn, develop and grow, the process should ultimately become quite natural.

Executed without ego, a listening tour bridges gaps, instills confidence and evokes kinship between departments and teams. Many benefits - as a result of smarter, more deliberate and strategic decision-making - become apparent almost instantly, while others - like advocacy and out-of-sight support - rise up over time. The up-front investment of time, caring and listening pays off and is practically self-sustaining. Throw in routine comeback tours and special engagements and you become the collaboration rock-star.

All from *simply* listening.

Listening Tour Cheat Sheet
1. Read *The Magical Listening Tour*
2. Embrace the importance of listening
3. Identify your **why**: Why are you doing this?
4. Introduce yourself
5. Schedule and show up
6. Prompt, then listen
7. Reflect on/document what you heard
8. Formulate action, "Did I hear you right?", solidify plan and share
9. Do the things
REPEAT